Bible Manhunt

Bible Manhunt

J. Curtis Manor

BAKER BOOK HOUSE
Grand Rapids, Michigan 49506

Copyright 1980 by
Baker Book House Company

ISBN: 0-8010-6097-4

Printed in the United States of America

Foreword

Bible Manhunt has been for several years one of the regular feature columns in *The World Evangelist*. This intriguing and challenging column is indeed a *feature*. It is unusual and very distinctive.

Fifty of the columns are in this book. These challenging riddles are a unique Bible study guide. They have already encouraged much learning of the Word of God, and this book will continue to stimulate the study of Bible truths.

Basil Overton, Editor
The World Evangelist
Florence, Alabama
June 1, 1979

How to Use this Book

This is not a book for children.

It is designed to challenge the knowledge and skill of the advanced Bible student, and to stimulate a more careful reading of the Scriptures; to provoke an appreciation of the importance of detail in God's message, and of the value of synthesis in studying it. . . . It is also designed to be fun!

Work on only one riddle at a time. Read it over to get a survey impression, then look carefully at the separate clues. Don't consider your search for the character ended until you can justify every clue with scripture or with well-known history. All clues are designed to coordinate with the King James Version of the Bible.

Only after you feel sure that you have "found your man" (or are honestly ready to give up the search) should you consult the solution at the end of the book.

Of the Bible personalities hidden in these fifty poems, most may be identified by name, but not all. There are men, women, and groups, good people and bad.

And now it's time to begin. Here's wishing you a successful manhunt. May you collect a rich bounty of increased knowledge of the Word of God!

J. Curtis Manor

1
The Riddler

I came to riddle the riddler,
To see if the riddler would,
By wisdom or wit, unriddle for me
My riddles, or if he could.[1]

    The riddler could, and would, and did
    Unriddle them, great and small;[2]
    And so I gave to him the prize:
    Gold, gems and spices, all.[3]

I traveled far[4] by train—not car—[5]
To verify the word;[6]
I had no thought of damning aught,
But will someday, you've heard.[7]

2
A Successful Failure

My name lent fame to a city small;[1]
    My strategy captured a fortress tall;[2]
You'll find I'm a patriarch, author and seer,[3]
    And at playing or fighting I've never a peer.[4]
My weapon, the greatest in Israel's band,
    Was not made for me: it was mine second hand.[5]

My spouses were many;[6] my children brought grief
    To me and my people;[7] for one, life was brief.[8]
For purpose deceptive I doodled and drooled:[9]
    Men thought me a traitor, but I kept
      them fooled.[10]

Three sins I committed against the Lord God,[11]
    And twice felt the wrath of his chastening rod.[12]
In faithful obedience I've seldom an equal;[13]
    In latter-day writ you may read of my sequel.[14]

My greatest ambition I failed to fulfill,[15]
    Yet I'm a success: I'll be honored until
The earth is no more, so great is my fame.[16]
    Now, with all of these clues,
      can you guess my name?

3
The Genealogist

My father is my cousin, by an oddity you'll see
If you ever take the trouble to trace out my family tree;
For father wed his auntie, so my great-aunt is
    my mother,[1]
Which makes me cousin once removed to sister
    and to brother.[2]
        Though siblings we,
        Yet this you'll see
If you look up my family tree!

To my two sons I'm also second cousin, don't you see,
Because of this coincidence of consanguinity;[3]
To mother I am grandnephew as well as favored son,[4]
And she's my children's great-grandaunt and
    grandmother in one.[5]
        Complexity,
        You'll sure agree,
If you check out my family tree![6]

When you consider my degree of kinship to myself,[7]
And think these things confusing, you don't
    comprehend the half!
So you begin to realize how wise the legislation
Which I proclaimed to others to curtail
    such conjugation;[8]
        Now, thanks to me,
        From kinks you're free
When you compute your family tree![9]

4
A Ubiquitous Prodigy

No matter where you'd go or dwell,
My speech you'd understand quite well;[1]
And yet, you might not comprehend
The gist of what I spoke or penned.[2]
Of all the places where I've been,
One might be bad, but never mean.[3]
A prodigy who traveled far,[4]
I did it all without a car;[5]
But should you purchase one for me,
You'd likely choose a Mercury.[6]

5

The Object Lesson

I never thought I'd see the day,[1]
But did, before the night,
Before the night of darkness came
To take away the light.[2]
     I sat in my accustomed place[3]
     While passers-by discussed my case,[4]
     Then hurried with anointed face
To prove the Maker's might.[5]

I readily espoused the cause
Of one I'd never seen,
Confounding arguments of those
Whose aim was to demean.[6]
     I had my say that holy day,[7]
     Then went upon my lonely way;[8]
     But soon I found a friend for aye
Who knew where I had been.[9]

6

The Kinsman

Think of many, think of much;[1]
Think of grassy plains and such.[2]
Think of a group, or a whole collection;[1]
I'm free because of a blood connection.[3]
Think of fortune, caste, position;[1]
I got in the way of a deadly mission.[4]
Think about a gambler's chance;[1]
My words incited jeers and rants.[5]
Think of a place to build a house;[1]
Think of a still and silent spouse;[6]
Surely, by now you understand,
I have two sons, and both are grand.[7]

7
The Last Word

The "famous last word"
From me[1] you have heard
Repeated by angel and men,[2]
For I foretold prophets yet scheduled to come
To turn folk to goodness from sin.[3]

I spoke of divorce—
Against it, of course—[4]
And wickedness,[5] love,[6] and of hate;[7]
And of sanctified fruit
Men were prone to pollute[8]
While indolence tended the gate.[9]

I foresaw the day
When judgment holds sway,
And the arrogant wicked decline;[10]
When God takes a look
In his memory book,
And the righteous like jewels shall shine.[11]

8

The Disconnected

Nineteen times my name is inflected
By readers of Scripture selected;[1]
With evil, not good, I'm connected,
Because from the right I defected.[2]

Intended to rule, I'm subjected,[3]
And so, by the Lord I'm rejected;
Yet under his care I'm protected,[4]
A fate better than I expected
Whenever my sin was detected.[5]
Too bad I could not be corrected.[6]

My exile my children affected:
A new kind of home I erected
When, far from my kin and dejected,
A new way of life I elected.[7]

One lesson from me is extracted:
God's statutes must not be neglected,[8]
For those who with sin are infected
Are ever from God disconnected![9]

9
The Lodger

My name is the same as my landlord's;
    We dwell in a house by the sea.[1]
        When I fain would pray,
        I'm summoned away[2]
By strangers[3] in search of a key.[4]

10

The Vanquished

Think about these matters odd:
Served by men who bore the hod,[1]
Pestered sore by creeping sod,[2]
Nostrils smote by stench like cod;[3]
Chastened by an alien rod,[4]
Vanquished by a servant's God,[5]
Just because I failed to nod![6]
Do you know me, and where I trod?[7]

11
The Poor Relation

Born at Bethlehem long ago,[1]
Exactly when, you'll never know;
Not in messianic line—[2]
Just a kinsman's lot is mine.
Although rife with progeny,[3]
Most perished due to sin, you see,[4]
In remnant leaving a satellite
Near a people of greater might.[5]

The lines of this foregone refrain
Declare my name in language plain.[6]

12

Related Rival

My aunt became my mother-in-law:[1]
    My cousin was my spouse,[2]
Which made complex relationships
    For members of our house.[3]

My sister was my "wife-in-law,"
    If you know what I mean;[4]
But I produced the favored sons,[5]
    Though one I've scarcely seen.[6]

13
The Dropout

Ten workers for God in the capital served:[1]
    Myself and my better-known friends;[2]
In company of Jesus[3] and of three who
   Scripture wrote,[4]
    I labored toward the holiest of ends.[5]

Our team dispersed to other fields,
    Except for those restrained[6]
And one who ever close at hand
    For friendly aid remained.[7]

But, although others left to serve,[8]
    I went my selfish way,
Pursuing lesser goals and base,
    For more immediate pay.[9]

14
The Picnicker

The Lord gave a sign for my sake,
To prove my opponent a fake;[1]
And when I was crying
And wished to be dying,[2]
He fed me with angel food cake![3]

15
The Intimidator

One time I intended to slaughter my son;
    It wasn't from hatred or malice:[1]
If I could have had the desire of my heart
    He would have been heir to a palace.[2]

I mustered an army without any arms,
    Through power of intimidation;[3]
But God gave us vict'ry with tools from our farms[4]
    And granted our kin liberation.[5]

Though great, I grew small;[6] though small,
    I grew great,[7]
    And routed the forces oppressing;[8]
But I sinned against God when the preacher was late,
    And forfeited favor and blessing.[9]

When I slept, my people divided;[10]
    If you know me you won't deny,
As hist'ry long since has decided.
    My namesake is greater than I.[11]

16
The Big Loser

Since I'm so much bigger,
You'd normally figure
That I would be stronger in battle;[1]
But my lesser foemen
Could be stopped by no men,[2]
And so they got all of my cattle.[3]

Leaving me dead,
They took pride in my stead,[4]
And gave my domain to the half clan;[5]
For livestock can grow
In this country, you know;
Especially a sheep or a calf can.[6]

I'm the end of a line[7]
In the country of kine,[8]
For the word of the Lord is no slack word,[9]
And our evil is full
In this land of the bull.[10]
This hint may assist you: Go backward.[11]

17

The Most Wanted Man

Of all my tribe, to fame
I alone can lay a claim,[1]
Though the way of God and fathers I forsook;[2]
And the price upon my head
Was the highest ever paid—
If you doubt it, you may check it in the Book.[3]

From my sheltered rocky home[4]
I was wont to safely roam,
Undismayed by friendly foe[5] or foe-ly friend;[6]
But my middle-aged affinity
For alien femininity
Allured me to my downfall in the end.[7]

I'm mean and tough and churlish,[8]
But no match for graces girlish,[9]
So, altho' I knew the ropes,[10] they caught me nappin';[11]
With malice diabolical
They stole my issues follicle,[12]
And after that the worst was bound to happen![13]

18
Man of Mystery

I'm greater than the father, though I do not have
    an heir;[1]
I'm closer than the friend, though accounts of me
    are rare;[2]
The record of my birth isn't found in all the earth,[3]
But my lack of pedigree simply multiplies my worth,
For that is why I'm chosen from among the saints
    who trod
The righteous path of old as being like the
    Son of God.[4]

19
The Survivor

Twice in my lifetime did God intervene
To counter the evils of men;[1]
Yet saints were supreme at a time in between,
Outnumb'ring the doers of sin.[2]

A builder and planter and preacher am I,
And conservationist, too;[3]
Unless you're a fish, you'd probably wish
That I were related to you![4]

20
The Chosen One

My second name means I'm beloved of God,[1]
But I'm better known by another.[2]
My father had many a son before me,[3]
But I'm second-born to my mother.[4]

Two brothers had I who were living; one, dead.[5]
A great granddad turned against father;
A traitor was he, and 'twould have ruined me
If he had succeeded,[6] but rather,

I gained my desserts,[7] and though I'm recalled
As a peaceable man in my day,[8]
My earlier years saw much violence and tears;
'Twas needful to 'stablish my sway.[9]

21
The One and Only

My name suggests my royalty;[1]
You'd judge me not unfair to be;[2]
Though some find me vindictive,[3]
The Bible calls me holy,[4]
For I believed that God is true,
Although he may work slowly.[5]

I gave my child a name of mirth
To celebrate his long-sought birth.[6]
I lived to see my son full-grown,
But not to see him wed,[7]
And yet my life affected his
Long after I was dead.[8]

Of all my kind in earth or heaven,
I am the one whose span is given.[9]

22

Wordy but Silent

No speech of mine's recorded,
Yet my words are quite prolific;[1]
Most learned of the saints save one,
My field is scientific.[2]
Renowned in song and story
Is the place from whence I come—[3]
Whence faith and service led me
Till I came at last to Rome.[4]
Just one more named in new writ[5]
Shares my occupation's title.[6]
—If you've not guessed my name by now,
Your brain in surely idle!

23
The Side-Kick

From my fickle native city[1] to the place a goddess fell,[2]
You may learn of my adventures if you're wise;[3]
For you'll trace me in the shadows while the sacred
  spotlights dwell
On another, who was full of enterprise.[4]
Though a half-breed[5] and a convict,[6] I have righteous
  friends galore;[7]
When God helps me, he's helping you.[8] Need I tell
  you more?

24
The Usurper

I got my name from what I am[1]
    Before I got to be it.[2]
I'm told my seed would overcome,
    But didn't live to see it.[3]

I'm of, and from, and for, and to,
    And with.[4]—That's how God meant me![5]
But now my offspring oft are found
    Where God's will never sent me![6]

Although I started from beside,[7]
    I soon assumed the lead;[8]
But many might be better off
    Had I not done my deed.[9]

God blessed me most abundantly,[10]
    Yet some deplore my lack.[11]
The night before the morning next
    Should put you on my track![12]

25
The Braggart

A fearsome, deadly clan were we:
    Five brothers[1] (One was odd)[2]
Who fought against one enemy[3]
    Who served a different God.[4]

My mail was sent to my enemy's tent,
    But not by my direction,[5]
For I lost my head,[6] and my comrades all fled
    In the interest of their own protection.[7]

Secure on the mountain, I boasted my race,
    For blustering speeches are free;
But down in the valley I fell on my face
    In shameful ignominy.[8]

In his very first battle my foeman faced me;[9]
    In his last one he fought with my brother;
And where I had failed, my kin had prevailed
    Had our foe not been saved by another![10]

26
The Rover

From Zion's proud city,[1]
From mother and home,[2]
To Paphos[3] and Salamis,[4]
Syria[5] and Rome[6]
And other far regions[7]
I go and I come;[8]
With Paul and with Peter
I labor and roam,[9]
And you'll find my mark[10]
In the heavenly tome.[11]
—Can you recognize me
From reading this poem?

27
The Spectator

Two brother men of Abrahamic line
In competition sought to gain my ear.[1]
Though neither trod the way the Jews call fine,[2]
Yet both had words they wanted me to hear.[3]

Each of them paid respect to Jesus' name,
As master, or as Savior, or as father;[4]
Still, when this day of confrontation came,
They found no common ground with one another.[5]

Both Hebrews undertook to help me see,
But each one to the other proved a bother;[6]
So, while the one brought greater light to me,
He gave a deeper darkness to the other.[7]

Now, if you know the men of whom I'm speaking,
You'll have no trouble spotting me, I know;[8]
So close the book: you've found the man
    you're seeking;
Just write my name upon the line below.

28

The Faithful Nephew

I'm a nephew to a king;[1]
He's the one who liked to sing![2]
I fight his battles far from home
While he enjoys his fling.[3]

I loved him like a son did[4]
—In fact, much more than one did;[5]
When rebels challenged Uncle's throne
I fought them off 'til none did.[6]

I'm not overly religious,[7]
But my courage is prodigious,[8]
And both God and sov'reign use me,
So my office is prestigious.[9]

My loyalty's unswerving
While my uncle-king I'm serving,
But fidelity's requited
With a cut I'm not deserving.[10]

29
The Answer

What knocking at yon portal breaks
Into our saintly prayer?[1]
I needs must go and silence it.
And see who may be there.[2]

For saints must not distracted be
From supplications fervent,
Directed to the throne of God
For his imperiled servant.[3]

Who is it? No! It cannot be!
My senses must be straying;[4]
God surely hasn't answered yet—
We haven't finished praying![5]

30
A Famous Cousin

You know me because of my cousin,
Though famous I've now come to be;[1]
    I outlived my brother;[2]
    My aunt became my mother,[3]
And father's name will rhyme here: _____ .[4]

31
The Youngest

One distinction I share with a woman;[1]
    Another I share with a man;[2]
Still another I share with no one,
    Because of my place in God's plan.[3]

I'm first or I'm not, all depending
    On how you are looking at me;[4]
A town bears my name, but no person,
    Though one's called by it figuratively.[5]

My spouse and my offspring brought sorrow
    And grief to my life and my clan;[6]
If you'd seek for me 'mongst my people,
    Just search for the youngest man.[7]

32
A Man of Rare Experience

'Twas in the year three-sixty-five;
No other man is yet alive
Who saw me walk in faith the way
That leads to ever-glorious day;[1]
But someday one will come from heaven
To judge those generations seven,[2]
With myriad saints,[3] in righteous mood
To damn the bad[4] and claim the good.[5]

33
The Voice of Prophecy

Some scholars call them "silent years,"
    When inspiration rested,[1]
But you'll know better, if you look
And read my story in the Book;
For upon me and more besides,
The supernatural gift abides,
    And so was manifested.[2]

My eyes have seen the glory
    Of the coming of the Lord;[3]
My hand has touched, my voice addressed,[4]
And future plan of God expressed;[5]
Of ups and downs,[6] of joy[7] and pain,[8]
But no one present could explain
    My dark and cryptic word.[9]

34
The Followers

Over the river and through the hills,
          To many a town we go;[1]
O'er many a year and many a mile
          We sally to meet our foe.[2]

We are young, but our leader is old,[3]
          And moved by the Spirit of God;[4]
So follow we must, if in God is our trust,[5]
          To places our fathers have trod.[6]

35
The Achiever

I am not a man of battle,
Nor a lord of sheep or cattle,[1]
But I'm wealthy[2] and I'm righteous,[3]
Though I have been known to tattle.[4]

Boastfulness gave way to patience
Through long years of tribulations,[5]
And the providence of God used me
To bless both men and nations.[6]

With aristocratic wife,[7]
And with wealth and honors rife,[8]
You'd not suspect the many wrongs
I've suffered in my life.[9]

36
Moral Support

My name is in fashion with parents today,[1]
For I'm talented, favored and famous.[2]
Among those inspired you will find me to be,[3]
Though I'm not an Isaiah nor an Amos.[4]

My moral support was right urgently sought,[5]
And given, with one stipulation,[6]
As up to the mountain we mustered,[7] but fought
In the valley against a great nation.[8]

Though greatly outnumbered, we struggled in faith,[9]
And God used the heavens and helped us[10]
To make our way safe, whether highroad or path,
From the foe who in terror had kept us.[11]

37
The Un-Prisoner

In prison, but never arrested;[1]
Enchained, but not for a charge;[2]
Released, though I would have protested
If I'd had a chance to enlarge.[3]

Restrained, but not in detention;[4]
Arraigned, but not for my deeds;[5]
Slaughtered for work of another—
I know not from whom it proceeds.[6]

Not guilty, though sentenced as if so,
With others, my comrades, to die.
When questioned, we knew not the answers,
So doom was our lot.[7] Who am I?

38
The Shadow

I jingle when I walk,[1] and I sparkle when I work;[2]
I'm a shadow[3] you can hear, and smell, and see.[4]
You can find me with your nose, and you'll know
    me by my clothes;[5]
My job depends upon my family tree.[6]

39
Double Agent

I saw a star that boded ill
For those who were my clients;[1]
With open eyes and open mouth[2]
I testified compliance
With godly plan and righteousness,[3]
But for my remuneration
I posed a plot to gain the ends
Of those I'd chosen as my friends[4]
By instigating evil trends
By means of fraternization.[5]

40
The Persister

Though wealthy, at farming I labored;[1]
    Four times I was told to remain,[2]
        But insistence at last brought fruition
            To the great hope that I entertained.[3]

I told the truth with the force of a lie,
And a nation received a new ruler thereby,[4]

My leader was hairy;[5] my follower, white.[6]
    I was greedy for favor with God,[7]
        And His revelation and mercy and might
            Attended the ways that I trod.[8]

If you need a cook, or an engineer,
Adviser, physician, predictor, I'm here![9]

My enemies sought my abduction,[10]
    But I o'ercame evil with good:
        I spared them, and led them, and fed them,
            And sent them home sated with food.[11]

If you e're float a loan you may think of me;[12]
Among seven thousand you'll find me to be.[13]

41

Man with an Alias

From telling tolls[1] to telling souls[2]
And scribing script for greater goals,[3]
The alteration of my name
Marks out my path[4] from shame[5] to shame;[6]
But God's appraisal's not the same,[7]
And he the future holds![8]

42
Obliging Spouse

I'm one of eight children you'll read of,[1]
But I'm the best-known of the lot;
For marriage brought fame,
And connected my name
With God's great and wonderful plot.[2]

My husband's a stranger;[3] he sent me away,
But soon I rejoined him for good;[4]
I once saved his life,
Like a dutiful wife,
Then reproached him in critical mood.[5]

43
The First and Second Choice

The Savior's orchestration
    Of the opus of salvation
        Required a virtuoso
            On the second violin.[1]

He called a man of substance,
    Compassion, and compliance,[2]
        And filled him full of grace
            To bring the sound of hope to men.[3]

He placed him in the lead
    Until a greater he could breed,[4]
        Then, trading parts betwixt the two,
            Achieved a better blend.[5]

44
The Rescuer

"They do him wrong!
They do him wrong!"
I cried unto the king;[1]
So he bid me fly
And hoist the man high
With padding of clothing and string.[2]

And thus a black man
Saved a white
From plots that the wicked were trying;[3]
And so, though a stranger,
God kept me from danger
When even the children were dying.[4]

45
The Fugitive

Over the river and through the hills,
To Grandfather's house did I flee:
      Asylum I sought
      For the vengeance I'd wrought,
Lest someone take vengeance on me![1]

Out of the city, within the dale,
A monument tall I raised
      Lest I be forgotten
      When flesh shall lie rotten;
At least, by myself I'll be praised.[2]

Around the city and in the gates,
By flattering speeches and kisses
      I captured all hearts,[3]
      But mine gathered darts—
What a loathesome development this is![4]

Over the river and through the woods
We ventured, my charger and I.[5]
      I stayed, but he went
      ('Twas not my intent!),
So I had no choice but to die.[6]

Though praised and uplifted, exalted on high,
Promoted by many a friend;[7]
      And even though my
      Chief admirer was I,[8]
Still I hung my head in the end![9]

46
Fair Diplomat

Thru the stomach, they say,
To the heart is the way,
So I plied him with edibles fine;[1]
And soon came the day
When God opened the way
For His chosen one to be mine.[2]

In Judah twice wed,[3]
But my first mate is dead;[4]
And my sister-in-law bears my name;[5]
My son is obscure,
But his name you will sure
Recognize from another man's fame.[6]

Kidnapped in a raid,
But no ransom was paid,
For four hundred came to my rescue.[7]
I saved one man's skin,[8]
And another from sin—[9]
A wife simply does what she has to.

47
The Deserted One

My son was not my son; he rather was my father;[1]
He left me out of greed for greater fame.[2]
My efforts to allure him back were scarcely worth
   the bother.[3]
Another, greater, later bore his name.[4]

A sinner I,[5] though all along I worshipped
   Israel's God—
A mongrel sort of worship, not the same
As what the Lord commanded: beyond his law I trod.[6]
A greater later also wore my name.[7]

48
First and Last

You'd know me because of my hairdo,[1]
And some of the clothes that I wear, too;[2]
I slept in a tent,
And served for my rent—[3]
At times, even more than I care to![4]

A part of my story is winsome;[5]
I served for a lifetime, and then some;[6]
When I went to pray,
My foes picked a fray;[7]
It's been a while now since there've been some![8]

I'm first and I'm last of my orders,
And famous from border to border;[9]
My offspring for long
Rendered praises in song,[10]
But I'm said to be a recorder![11]

49
The Sprinter

"O Runner! O Runner! Wherefore do you fly?
 Beware that you run not so swiftly as I!"[1]
My father forever in me you will see,[2]
 But ere you can spot him, you'll have to find me![3]
My young men, they played at a hazardous game.[4]
 For years in the papers you noticed my name.[5]

50
The Poor Loser

My home sounds like Shiloh, but isn't;[1]
In station I'm more than a peasant;[2]
    But, exalted in life,
    I was higher in death:
My demise was far less than pleasant.[3]

You'd call me a poor sport, I'm sure,
Yet one thing I just can't endure:
    Fools spurn wise advice;
    But one thing is nice:
They'll get none of mine, evermore![4]

My name is not to hard to spell;
Just write it here: _____ .[5]

Solutions

1. The Queen of Sheba — I Kings 10

[1] King Solomon was a "riddler"—a writer of proverbs and "dark sayings" (Prov. 1:6). The Queen of Sheba came "to prove him with hard questions" (I Kings 10:1).

[2] She was unable to stump the wise king with any of her questions (I Kings 10:3).

[3] Her gifts are noted in I Kings 10:10.

[4] ". . . from the uttermost parts of the earth . . ." (Matt. 12:42).

[5] Camel train (I Kings 10:2).

[6] She came to investigate the report she had heard of Solomon's wisdom and splendor (I Kings 10:6, 7).

[7] Jesus said, "The queen of the south shall rise up in the judgment with this generation, and shall condemn it: for she came from the uttermost parts of the earth to hear the wisdom of Solomon; and, behold, a greater than Solomon is here" (Matt. 12:42).

Note: The author gratefully acknowledges the collaboration of DeNell Stoppelman in the composition of this riddle.

2. David, psalmist and king

[1] Bethlehem, "little among the thousands of Judah" (Mic. 5:2), was known as "the city of David" (Luke 2:4).

[2] Jerusalem (II Sam. 5:6-9), the mountaintop city (Isa. 2:1-3).

[3] See Acts 2:29, 30; I Sam. 9:9. He was the author of many of the Psalms.

[4] For his musical talents, see I Sam. 16:16-23; for his military prowess, I Sam. 18:7.

[5] He carried the great sword he had taken from the giant Goliath (I Sam. 21:8-9).

[6] His wives and concubines are listed in I Chron. 3:1-9 and II Sam. 5:13.

[7] In fulfillment of Nathan's prophecy (II Sam. 12:10-11). See accounts in II Sam. 13, 15, 18, etc.

[8] The ill-begotten son of David and Bathsheba died in infancy (II Sam. 12:15-18).

[9] He feigned idiocy at Gath (I Sam. 21:10-15).

[10] The Philistines believed David to be plundering his own people when he looted the Amalekite outposts (I Sam. 27:7-12).

[11] Adultery (II Sam. 11:3-4), murder (II Sam. 12:9), and the taking of an unlawful census (II Sam. 24:10).

[12] The taking of the infant child in reprisal for the first two sins (II Sam. 12:15), and the three-day pestilence for the third (II Sam. 24:10-25).

[13] By God's own evaluation (I Kings 15:5).

[14] Jesus Christ, the Son of David, in the New Testament Scriptures (Matt. 21:9).

[15] He wished to build the house of the Lord, but was restrained from doing so (I Chron. 22:6-11).

[16] Do you doubt it?

3. Moses, the lawgiver

[1] "And Amram took him Jochebed His father's sister to wife; and she bare him Aaron and Moses" (Exod. 6:20). This made Moses the son of his father's aunt, hence, his father's cousin. Also, as the father's aunt, Jochebed was her son's great-aunt.

²The child of one's great-aunt is a "first cousin once removed." Aaron and Miriam (I Chron. 6:3) occupied this position.

³Since the children of first cousins are "second cousins" to each other, and Moses was his father's first cousin, as explained above.

⁴Since she was his father's aunt.

⁵The aunt of their grandfather, Amram; the mother of their father, Moses.

⁶Don't you?

⁷As the son of his father's aunt, and of his mother's nephew, he was his own cousin!

⁸The law of Moses forbade the intermarriage of such close relatives as Amram and Jochebed (Lev. 18:12).

⁹The laws regulating marriage among relatives which were first proclaimed by Moses have become the basis of taboos that are upheld by the legal systems of all civilized peoples today.

4. Paul, apostle of Jesus Christ to the Gentiles

¹Like the other apostles, Paul had the inspired ability to speak in foreign languages, or tongues, and professed to have made more extensive use of this ability than others (Cf. Acts 2:4-11; I Cor. 14:18).

²Though his language might be intelligible, the proper understanding of his meaning might sometimes require special thought and attention. His fellow apostle, Peter, commented that Paul, in his epistles, spoke "some things hard to be understood" (II Peter 3:15-16).

³He came from Tarsus, which he described as "no mean city" (Acts 21:39).

⁴He compares himself to "one born out of due time" (I Cor. 15:8), or out of the usual course of nature, and also speaks of having progressed beyond his peers among the Jews' religion (Gal. 1:14)—in either sense, a "prodigy." The extent of his missionary travels is, of course, proverbial.

⁵Naturally, he used the travel modes of his own time.

⁶An allusion to the occasion, recorded in Acts 14:11-12, when the people of Lystra mistook him for Mercurius, or Mercury, the mythological Roman messenger of the gods.

5. The man who was born blind, of John 9:1-38

¹He had no hope of sight: "Since the world began was it not heard that any man opened the eyes of one that was born blind" (v. 32).

²Jesus, who said, "As long as I am in the world, I am the light of the world" (v. 5), miraculously gave the man sight, commenting, "I must work . . . while it is day: the night cometh, when no man can work" (v. 4). He attributed his approaching crucifixion to "the power of darkness" (Luke 22:53).

³He habitually sat and begged (v. 8) near the temple (John 8:59-9:1).

⁴Jesus and his disciples noticed him as they passed by, and discussed the reason for his blindness (v. 1-3).

⁵Jesus proposed to use the man's blindness as an occasion to demonstrate the working of God (v. 3). Anointing his eyes with clay, he sent him to wash in the pool of Siloam. The man obeyed, and received his sight, thus "the works of God" were "made manifest in him" (v. 3, 6-7).

⁶Since he received his sight at the pool and not in the presence of Jesus, he had not seen the one who opened his eyes, yet he stoutly defended him against the calumny of the Pharisees (v. 13-17, 24-34).

⁷It was the sabbath day (v. 14).

⁸When he defended Christ, the Pharisees cast him out (v. 34) and others were afraid to stand by him, lest they be treated likewise (v. 22).

⁹Jesus, who had heard of his unjust treatment and sought him out (v. 35). He became a believer in him who said, "Him that cometh to me I will in no wise cast out" (John 6:37).

6. Lot, nephew of Abraham

[1]The first lines of the rhyming couplets refer to different meanings of the word "lot." "Many," "much," "group," "collection," "fortune," "caste," "position," "gambler's chance," or "place to build a house."

[2]Lot chose the well-watered plain of Jordan as a grazing ground for his cattle (Gen. 13:5-13).

[3]Lot was captured by the invading kings of Mesopotamia, but was set free in a daring raid by his uncle, Abraham (Gen. 14:1-16).

[4]The angel of the Lord could not proceed with his mission of destruction upon Sodom until Lot was safely evacuated. Read the story in Genesis 19, and note the angel's statement in verse 22.

[5]His plea on behalf of the guests in his house provoked abusive language from the threatening Sodomites (Gen. 19:6-9).

[6]Lot's wife became a pillar of salt (Gen. 19:26).

[7]His sons, Moab and Ben-Ammi, were also his grandsons, since they were borne by his daughters (Gen. 19:36-38).

7. The prophet Malachi

[1]Malachi was the last of the Old Testament writers.

[2]The closing words of Malachi's prophecy were cited by the angel who appeared to Zacharias to announce the impending birth of John the Baptist (Mal. 4:5-6; Luke 1:17), and alluded to by the disciples of Jesus (Mark 9:11). Malachi was also quoted by Zacharias himself (Mal. 3:1; Luke 1:76).

[3]Namely, John the Baptist, as noted above, and Jesus himself (Mal. 3:1; 4:2).

[4]"For the Lord, the God of Israel, saith that he hateth putting away" (Mal. 2:14-16).

[5]See Mal. 1:4.

[6]See Mal. 1:2.

[7] See Mal. 1:3.

[8] See Mal. 1:7, 12.

[9] See Mal. 1:10, 13.

[10] See Mal. 4:1-3.

[11] See Mal. 3:16-18.

8. Cain, eldest son of Adam and Eve

[1] His name appears in the Bible nineteen times. Check any complete concordance.

[2] God cursed him for having murdered his brother, Abel (Gen. 4:9-12).

[3] He was told to rule over sin, but instead he allowed it to rule him (Gen. 4:7-8).

[4] God drove him into exile, but set a mark on him to protect his life against possible avengers (Gen. 4:14-15).

[5] He knew he deserved to die, and expected someone to kill him (4:14).

[6] How much better had he heeded God's warning and "done well," ruling over the sin which "lay at his door" (4:7).

[7] Since he could no longer farm effectively (Gen. 4:12), he built a city—the first mentioned in the Bible—and reared his children as city dwellers (4:17). Significantly, the earliest practitioners of the urban pursuit of metalworking are named among his descendants (4:22).

[8] The lesson is repeated countless times, cf. Deuteronomy 28:15.

[9] That is, unless and until that infection is cleansed (Isa. 1:18; Acts 13:38-39).

9. Simon Peter, apostle of Christ

[1] Simon Peter was lodging in the home of another "Simon," a tanner, "whose house is by the sea side" in Joppa (Acts 10:1-6).

²Peter had gone up to the housetop to pray when messengers arrived to escort him to Caesarea (Acts 10:9-21).

³The men were Gentiles, commonly called "strangers" by the Jews (Cf. Luke 17:18; Eph. 2:12, 19).

⁴The Gentiles had come in search of the gospel of Christ (Acts 11:14)—"words" whereby they might be saved. God was ready to open "the door of faith to the Gentiles" (Acts 14:27), and Jesus had entrusted to Peter the "keys" (Matt. 16:19). Thus, as Peter had been first to proclaim the resurrected Christ to the Jews (Acts 2:22-41), opening the door of the kingdom to them, he was now summoned to perform a like service for the Gentiles. Read the entire tenth and eleventh chapters of Acts, and compare Acts 15:7-11, 14.

10. Pharaoh, king of Egypt at the time of the Exodus—Exodus 5-14

¹Pharaoh enslaved the Israelites and put them to work making bricks (Exod. 5:5-8). The hod is a sort of tray used for carrying bricks.

²In one of the ten plagues which God inflicted upon him and his people, the dust of the ground became lice (Exod. 8:15-17).

³The first of the plagues was attended by the odor of dead fish (Exod. 7:20-21).

⁴God used a wooden rod in the hands of Aaron, a Hebrew, to bring the chastening plagues upon the Egyptian king (Exod. 7:17-20; 8:5, 16, etc.).

⁵He conceded defeat (Exod. 30-32) at the hands of the Lord God of Israel—the God of his slaves, whom he had held in contempt (Exod. 5:1-2).

⁶God's wrath was poured out upon Pharaoh because of his refusal to honor God's demands (Exod. 7:2-5).

⁷He was Pharaoh, and he trod in Egypt.

11. Benjamin, youngest son of Jacob

[1] "there was but a little way to come to Ephrath: and Rachel travailed. . . . And Rachel died, and was buried in the way to Ephrath, which is Bethlehem" (Gen. 35:16-19). The date is uncertain.

[2] "it is evident that our Lord sprang out of Judah" (Heb. 7:14). Judah was Benjamin's half-brother (Gen. 35:22-24).

[3] Ten sons of Benjamin are numbered among those who migrated to Egypt (Gen. 46:21), more than any of his brothers had. His tribe grew to be one of the largest, by the time of Moses' census (Num. 2).

[4] The tribe was all but wiped out in the fratricidal war occasioned by the atrocities of the Benjamites of Gibeah against a traveling Levite and his wife. The story covers chapters 19 through 21 of the book of Judges.

[5] Surviving as the smallest tribe in Israel (I Sam. 9:21), Benjamin, in later history, shared the territory and fortunes of the dominant tribe of Judah (I Kings 12:20-23).

[6] Read down the initials of the lines. The poem is an acrostic, spelling out the name.

12. Rachel, beloved wife of Jacob

[1] Rachel was the daughter of Laban (Gen. 29:5-6), who was the brother of Rebekah (Gen. 24:29). Rebekah was the mother of Jacob (Gen. 27:6), who married Rachel (Gen. 29:28).

[2] Obviously, from the relationships noted above.

[3] For instance, her son would also be her first cousin once removed, brothers would be cousins, their grandmother would also be an aunt, etc.

[4] Jacob was married to the two sisters, Leah and Rachel (Gen. 29:16-30). If a husband's brother is a "brother-in-law," wouldn't a husband's other wife be a "wife-in-law"?

[5]Rachel was Jacob's preferred wife (Gen. 29:30), and her two sons, Joseph and Benjamin, also enjoyed his special partiality (Gen. 37:3; 42:3-4).

[6]Though she died in giving birth to Benjamin, she apparently lived long enough to know he was a boy, and to give him a name (Gen. 35:18).

13. Demas, who forsook the apostle Paul—II Timothy 4:10

[1]In the letter to the Colossians, the apostle Paul refers to ten Christians who were laboring for the Lord in Rome at the time. The list included Paul and Timothy (Col. 1:1), Tychicus, Onesimus, Aristarchus, Marcus, Jesus Justus, Epaphras, Luke and Demas (Col. 4:7-14).

[2]The company included such familiar personalities as Paul, Timothy, Mark and Luke.

[3]"Jesus, which is called Justus" (Col. 4:11).

[4]Namely, Paul, Mark and Luke, all of whom wrote parts of the New Testament scriptures.

[5]As a fellow worker with Paul (Philem. 24). Demas was engaged in the work of salvation.

[6]Paul tells of it in II Timothy 4:9-12. Excluded from the dispersion, of course, would be those of the number who were prisoners.

[7]Luke, "the beloved physician," remained with the imprisoned apostle Paul (II Tim. 4:11; Col. 4:14).

[8]Their missions are revealed in Colossians 4:7-9 and II Timothy 4:1-2, 11.

[9]Unlike those who were sent on missions, Demas forsook the apostle, "having loved this present world," and "departed unto Thessalonica" (II Tim. 4:10).

14. The prophet Elijah—I Kings 18-19

[1] When Elijah was challenging the power of the false god, Baal, he prayed to God, "Lord God of Abraham, Isaac and of Israel, let it be known this day that thou art God in Israel, and that I am thy servant . . ." God responded by sending a supernatural fire to consume Elijah's sacrifice (I Kings 18:36, 38).

[2] Threatened by Jezebel after his victory over Baal, Elijah fled into the desert and prayed for death (I Kings 19:1-4).

[3] Instead of granting his request, God sent an angel, who fed Elijah with "a cake baken on the coals" and a cruse of water (I Kings 19:5-6).

15. Saul, first anointed king of Israel

[1] He was about to kill his son, Jonathan, in fulfillment of a sacred oath when the people intervened (I Sam. 14:24-27, 36-45).

[2] He wished for his son to inherit the kingdom after him. This was one factor in his resentment against David (I Sam. 20:30-31).

[3] He threatened to slaughter the cattle of all who failed to heed his summons (I Sam. 11:7-8). 330,000 men responded. They had no weapons of war, because the Philistines had disarmed the Israelites (I Sam. 13:19-22). It is presumed, therefore, that they fought with the tools of peace.

[4] The goads, mattocks, axes and forks referred to in 13:20-21.

[5] Saul's first military effort was a battle of liberation on behalf of the Trans-Jordan Israelite village of Jabesh-Gilead (I Sam. 11:1-11).

[6] In God's estimation. The Lord exalted him and gave him success, then rejected him when he became rebellious (I Sam. 13:13-14; 15:23).

[7] In his own eyes (I Sam. 15:17). He exalted himself to the point of defying God's will (I Sam. 15:19, 22-26).

⁸ Saul was victorious over the oppressive Philistines and other enemies of Israel (I Sam. 14:46-48).

⁹ When the prophet Samuel did not appear at the time appointed to offer sacrifice, Saul presumptuously did so. This marked the beginning of his alienation from God (I Sam. 13:8-14).

¹⁰ Upon the death of Saul, his kingdom divided, part going to David and part supporting his son, Ish-bosheth (II Sam. 2:4, 8-10).

¹¹ Who would deny that Saul of Tarsus was a greater man than Saul the son of Kish?

16. Og, king of Bashan—Numbers 21:33-35

¹ Og was a giant (Deut. 3:11).

² Divine assistance made the Israelist army invincible so long as the people remained obedient to God. His promise: "there shall no man be able to stand before thee" (Deut. 7:24).

³ See Deuteronomy 3:7.

⁴ After the slaughter of Og, his "bedstead of iron" was exhibited in the city of Rabaath, probably as a war trophy (Deut. 3:11).

⁵ The territory of his kingdom was allotted to the half tribe of Manasseh (Deut. 3:13).

⁶ Two and a half tribes chose to settle east of the Jordan because "the place was a place for cattle" (Num. 32:1, 33).

⁷ "only Og . . . remained of the remnant of giants (Deut. 3:11).

⁸ Bashan was famous for its cattle; the "bulls of Bashan" were proverbial (Cf. Ps. 22:12; Amos 4:1; Ezek. 39:18).

⁹ "The Lord is not slack concerning his promise" (II Peter 3:9).

¹⁰ God had promised this land to Abraham's seed when "the iniquity of the Amorites" should be full (Gen. 15:7, 15-18). That time had now come (Deut. 9:5). For "land of the bull," see above note on "country of kine."

¹¹ "G-O." Spell it backward: "O-G," "Og."

17. Samson, the strong man and judge of Israel—Judges 13-16

1 How many other names do you remember from the tribe of Dan? Most Bible readers do know of Manoah, but only because he is Samson's father (Judg. 13:2-5, 24).

2 He was not too fastidious about observing God's commandments. Examples may be found in his seeking a Philistine wife (Judg. 14:1-3), eating "unclean" food (14:8-9), patronizing a harlot (Judg. 16:1), etc.

3 The five lords of the Philistines each paid Delilah eleven hundred pieces of silver—a total reward of 5,500—to betray Samson into their hands (Judg. 16:5, 18; cf. Judg. 3:3; I Sam. 6:4). This appears to have been the highest price recorded in the Bible as the reward of treachery against one individual.

4 Samson "dwelt in the top of the rock Etam" (Judg. 15:11).

5 He seems to have traveled freely and unafraid among his enemies, the Philistines, who respected his great strength and, apparently, avoided direct confrontation with him as a rule.

6 His own people once turned him over to the Philistines to avoid suffering reprisal for his exploits against the heathen (Judg. 15:9-13).

7 He seems to have had a special fondness for Philistine women, rather than for the daughters of his own people (Judg. 14:1-3; 16:1, 4). This proved to be his undoing at the hands of Delilah (Judg. 16:4-17). He was by this time a man of mature years, having judged Israel for 20 years (Judg. 15:20).

8 Toward the Philistines, at any rate (Judg. 14:19; 15:3-8).

9 He couldn't resist the pouting wiles of Delilah (Judg. 16:15-17).

10 He had teased her by telling her different ways to bind him (Judg. 16:7, 11, etc.).

11 He was asleep on Delilah's lap when he was captured (Judg. 16:19).

12 That which issues from the follicle is hair; the Philistines shaved off his hair while he slept (Judg. 16:19).

¹³ When his hair was gone, so was his legendary strength, and he was helpless in the hands of his enemies (Judg. 16:19-21). Read his entire thrilling story in Judges 14-16.

18. Melchizedek, priest-king of Salem—Genesis 14:17-20

¹ The Bible accords Melchizedek greater prestige than Abraham, the "father of the faithful," since he was in a position to bless Abraham, and "the less is blessed of the better" (Heb. 7:4-7). This despite the fact that much of a man's honor was derived from a numerous progeny (Gen. 17:4-6), and Melchizedek is acknowledged to have been "without descent" (Heb. 7:3).

² He is mentioned only in Genesis 14:18-20, Psalms 110:4 and Hebrews 5-7, yet Abraham, who was the "friend of God" (II Chron. 20:7; Isa. 41:8), paid tithes to him as God's priest, thus acknowledging that Melchizedek occupied a position that was closer to God than his own.

³ "Without father, without mother . . . ." (Heb. 7:3).

⁴ It is this very independence of any human dynasty which makes his priesthood a fitting type of that of Jesus Christ, as pointed out in Hebrews 7:8-17.

19. Noah, Genesis 6-9

¹ God counteracted man's rebellion during Noah's lifetime first, by sending the flood to destroy the wicked (Gen. 6:13, 17), and, second, by confounding the people's speech and scattering them from the tower of Babel (Gen. 11:1-9). The first intervention took place when Noah was 599 years old (Gen. 7-11); the second, a little more than 100 years later. We are told that Peleg was named after the event (Gen. 10:25). The time of Peleg's birth may be computed from Genesis 11:10-16. Noah lived for 350 years after the flood, attaining the age of 950 years (Gen. 9:28-29).

² The wicked were all destroyed in the flood, leaving righteous Noah and his family in complete possession of the earth. Thus,

for a time, until sin got a fresh start, the righteous were in the majority—a position they have not enjoyed at any time since.

³He built an ark (Heb. 11:7), planted a vineyard (Gen. 9:20), preached righteousness (II Peter 2:5), and conserved breeding stock of all the earth's land creatures (Gen 7:2-3).

⁴Aquatic life was not endangered by the flood. Of land species, only the charges of Noah survived (Gen. 7:22-23). Of the human race, only those of his family (Gen. 7:1, 7).

20. Solomon, the wise king of Israel

¹David named his son Solomon, "and the Lord loved him. And he sent by the hand of Nathan the prophet; and he called his name Jedidiah, because of the Lord" (II Sam. 12:24-25).

²The name "Solomon" is used in all the Bible narrative of his exploits.

³At least seven. David's sons are listed in I Chron. 3:1-9.

⁴Bathsheba's first child by David died (II Sam. 12:15-24).

⁵David and Bathsheba had four sons: Shimea, Shobab, Nathan and Solomon (I Chron. 3:5). We do not know which of the first two was the short-lived infant who preceded Solomon.

⁶Ahithophel, David's trusted counselor who defected to Absalom's rebellion, appears to have been Bathsheba's grandfather (II Sam. 23:34; 11:3). If Absalom had followed Ahithophel's advice his rebellion probably would have succeeded, and Solomon would not have become king (II Sam. 16:23; 17:14. Cf. II Sam. 15:30-37; 16:15-17:23).

⁷Through the providence of God in this and other matters, Solomon did become king, as the Lord and his father David had intended (I Kings 2:12).

⁸See I Chron. 22:9; I Kings 4:24-25.

⁹Solomon's accession to the throne was marked by the violence of a blood purge due to unrest and rebellion during the last part of David's reign, and the enemies who challenged his throne.

Read the first two chapters of I Kings for an account of these troubles, and especially David's deathbed counsel to his son in 2:1-9.

21. Sarah, Abraham's wife

[1]Sarah: "Princess" *(Young's Analytical Concordance to the Bible).*

[2]In fact, she is described as "a fair woman to look upon" (Gen. 12:11, 14).

[3]Because of her treatment of Hagar and Ishmael (Gen. 16:6; 21:9-10).

[4]See I Peter 3:5-6.

[5]Her faith is attested in Hebrews 11:11.

[6]Her son was Isaac, "Laughter" *(Young's Analytical Concordance to the Bible);* "And Sarah said, God hath made me to laugh, so that all that hear will laugh with me" (Gen. 21:6).

[7]Sarah was ninety years old when she bore her son (Gen. 17:17). She died at the age of one hundred twenty-seven (Gen. 23:1-2), three years, therefore, prior to Isaac's marriage at age forty (Gen. 25:20).

[8]His mother's tent became the home of Isaac and his bride (Gen. 24:67).

[9]She is the only woman whose lifespan is recorded in the Bible (Gen. 23:1-2). Apparently, women have always been reluctant for their age to be known!

22. Luke, companion of Paul and author of Scripture

[1]Luke wrote the Gospel that bears his name and the Acts of the Apostles, two of the longest books of the New Testament, but there is no record of any spoken word of his.

[2]He was a physician (Col. 4:14); he may therefore be presumed to have received more formal education than any of the other New Testament personalities, with the probable exception of the apostle Paul, who attended the rabbinical school of Gamaliel (Acts 22:3), the ranking Jewish seminary of his day.

[3]Though tradition claims that Luke was born at Antioch, it was at Troas that Paul found him, and from there that he began his travels with the apostle. Notice the change in his narrative from third to second person in Acts 16:8-11. Troas was the ancient Troy of Greek legend and song.

[4]The latest reference to Luke that we have in the Scriptures is from Paul's pen while he was imprisoned at Rome: "Only Luke is with me" (II Tim. 4:11).

[5]The New Testament Scriptures

[6]Jesus Christ spoke of himself, figuratively, as a physician (Luke 4:23).

23. Timothy (Timotheus), protege and assistant of the apostle Paul

[1]Timothy apparently came from Lystra (Acts 16:1-2), a city whose people first hailed Paul and Barnabas as gods, then assaulted them and ran them out of town, stoning Paul and leaving him for dead (Acts 14:8-19).

[2]Ephesus, custodian city of the image of Diana, which the people believed to have fallen down from Jupiter (Acts 19:35).

[3]The earliest notice of Timothy is that of his recruitment by Paul at Lystra (Acts 16:1-3). The last definite location that we have for him is Ephesus: "As I besought thee to abide still at Ephesus. . . ." (I Tim. 1:3).

[4]References to Timothy and his activities are, for the most part, incidental to the career of the tireless apostle Paul who "laboured more abundantly than they all" (I Cor. 15:10).

[5]Timothy was the son of a Jewish mother and a Greek father (Acts 16:1).

[6]Hebrews 13:23 states that "our brother Timothy is set at liberty," so he apparently had been in prison.

[7]Paul, Luke, Mark, etc. (Col. 1:1; 4:7-14).

[8]The inspired Scriptures of First and Second Timothy were written to guide this young man in doing God's will; they are helpful to every Christian today for the same purpose (II Tim. 3:16-17).

24. Eve, the first woman

[1]"And Adam called his wife's name Eve; because she was the mother of all living" (Gen. 3:20). The name, according to *Young's Analytical Concordance to the Bible*, means "life," or "life-giving."

[2]She appears to have received the name before she had any children.

[3]God predicted that her seed would bruise the serpent's head (Gen. 3:14-15), a prophecy generally taken to refer to the victory of Christ, who was "made of a woman" (Gal. 4:4)—not of a man (Luke 1:30-35), over Satan, "the Old Serpent" (Rev. 12:9), which was destined to take place long after Eve's lifetime (Heb. 2:14).

[4]All these prepositions are used in the Scriptures to describe the woman's relationship to the man: "the woman is *of* the man" (I Cor. 11:8, 12). "And the rib, which the Lord God had taken *from* the man, made he a woman" (Gen. 2:22). "The woman whom thou gavest to be *with* me. . . ." (Gen. 3:12).

[5]The foregoing words express God's intent regarding the proper husband-wife relationship.

[6]That is, in a position of dominance over the husband, whether by feminist ambition or male abdication.

[7]She was made from Adam's rib, and was given to be "with" him (Gen. 2:24; 3:12).

[8]She was first to sample the forbidden fruit, and influenced her husband to follow her example (Gen. 3:6).

⁹ As a result of this action, sin entered the world, and death through sin (Rom. 5:12).

¹⁰ By endowing her with the distinctive charms of femininity and the exclusive capacity for motherhood (Gen. 3:20; I Cor. 11:12).

¹¹ "Many today regard women as "underprivileged," because of these very distinctions.

¹² "Eve," a word commonly used to designate the night before some special event: "New Year's Eve," "Christmas Eve," On the eve of the election," etc.

25. Goliath, the Philistine—I Samuel 17

¹ The warrior sons who were "born unto the giant in Gath (II Sam. 21:22; I Chron. 20:8). Four of them are identified by name in II Samuel 21:15-22 and I Chronicles 20:4-8: Ishbibenob, Saph (Sippai), Lahmi, and Goliath himself.

² The fifth brother is noted as having abnormal hands and feet, but his name is not revealed (II Sam. 21:20; I Chron. 20:6).

³ All were mortal enemies of David, and were all killed by him and his servants (II Sam. 21:22; I Chron. 20:8).

⁴ David, of course, served the Lord God of Israel, whereas the giants were pagan (I Sam. 17:43).

⁵ Goliath's armor, which included a massive coat of mail (I Sam. 17:5), was claimed as spoil of war and placed in David's tent (I Sam. 17:54).

⁶ David claimed it as a battle trophy (I Sam. 17:54, 57).

⁷ "when the Philistines saw their champion was dead, they fled" (I Sam. 17:51).

⁸ Contrast Goliath's arrogant challenge with his actual performance (I Sam. 17:3-10, 41-50).

⁹ The fight with Goliath was David's first military encounter (I Sam. 17:33-36).

[10] The battle in which he was saved from Goliath's brother, Ishbibenob, by the timely intervention of Abishai was David's last personal combat, by the concerned petition of his followers (II Sam. 21:15-17).

26. John Mark, writer of the second Gospel

[1] Jerusalem. Her pride is referred to by several of the Old Testament prophets (Ezek. 16:56; Zeph. 3:11).

[2] Mark was the son of Mary, a Christian woman of Jerusalem (Acts 12:12, 25).

[3] See Acts 13:6.

[4] See Acts 13:5.

[5] Antioch in Syria (Acts 15:23).

[6] See Philemon 23-24.

[7] As far as Babylon (I Peter 5:13).

[8] His "going" is noted in Acts 12:25; 13:4-5; his "coming" is related in Acts 13:13.

[9] He assisted Paul, as noted in the foregoing scripture references, and Peter closes his first epistle with salutations from himself, the church at Babylon, and "Marcus my son" (I Peter 5:13).

[10] "Mark," the second Gospel, is his work.

[11] The Bible, inspired word of God (II Tim. 3:16).

27. Sergius Paulus, the Roman deputy at Paphos, Cyprus—Acts 13:4-12

[1] Saul of Tarsus, a Jew (Acts 21:39), and Elymas the sorcerer, also a Jew, were both trying to instruct the deputy (Acts 13:7-8).

[2] Neither of Sergius' would-be advisers would have been regarded as a faithful Jew by his own people. Saul worshipped God "after

the way which they call heresy" (Acts 24:14), and Elymas was a sorcerer and a false prophet, in violation of the law of Moses (Deut. 18:9-12, 20).

3Saul wanted to teach him the doctrine of Christ, while Elymas withstood him, apparently fearful of losing his position of influence with the deputy should he become a Christian (Acts 13:7-8).

4Saul, of course, honored the name of Jesus as his Savior and Lord; Elymas, on the other hand, was the son of a man named Jesus, as indicated by his surname, "Bar-jesus," which thus honored his father (Acts 13:6).

5The "Jesus" each one honored was different; they opposed each other.

6Each sought to sway the deputy to his own view, but since they were at cross purposes they got in each other's way.

7In order to teach the deputy, or enlighten him, so that he became a believer, Saul silenced the competition of Elymas by invoking a curse of temporary blindness upon him. "And immediately there fell on him a mist and a darkness" (Acts 13:9-12).

8If you know enough to identify the two antagonists, you know that the deputy's name was Sergius Paulus, since the entire incident is recorded in one scripture passage.

28. Joab, commander-in-chief of King David's army

1Joab was a son of Zeruiah (II Sam. 8:16), who was a sister of David (I Chron. 2:15-16).

2David, the "sweet psalmist of Israel" (II Sam. 23:1).

3At the time of David's adulterous affair with Bathsheba, Joab was leading the king's army in a siege of Rabbah, capital city of the Ammonites (II Sam. 11:1-4).

4Joab's devotion to David is shown in many ways: by his concern for David's honor above his own (II Sam. 12:26-28), by his solicitude for the king's peace of mind (II Sam. 14:1-3), by his sympathy for his sorrow (II Sam. 18:19-20), and by his courage to give him needed, though unpleasant, counsel (II Sam. 19:5-7).

5 His love for David certainly surpassed that of Absalom, who publicly humiliated his father (II Sam. 16:20-22) and plotted against his life (II Sam. 17:1-4, 11-12).

6 Joab led David's loyal forces to victory over the rebellious Absalom and his followers (II Sam. 15:1-20:22).

7 Though faithful and loyal as a soldier, friend and counselor to David, Joab shows no significant evidence of personal piety. He refers to God as "the Lord thy God"—David's (II Sam. 24:3).

8 His moral courage is shown by his willingness to "talk back" to the king (II Sam. 19:5-7; 24:3). His physical courage was demonstrated on numerous occasions; for example, his daring assault upon the Jebusite stronghold of Zion (I Chron. 11:6).

9 God used him to protect David, and to implement the divine plan for Israel's success and glory. For example, it was he who led the Israelite forces in subjugating the neighboring lands of Syria, Edom, Moab and Ammon, thus extending Israel's rule to the areas originally promised to Abraham, as detailed in God's briefing of Joshua (Josh. 1:1-4; cf. II Sam. 8:1-16). David sometimes used him for services less noble, such as that of eliminating Uriah the Hittite (II Sam. 11:14-17).

10 David rewarded Joab's lifelong loyalty by demoting him from his command and giving it to an erstwhile enemy, Amasa (II Sam. 19:11-13).

29. Rhoda, a girl in the house of
Mary of Jerusalem—Acts 12:1-17

1 Many disciples were gathered at Mary's house in prayer, when a knock was heard at the door of the gate (Acts 12:12-13).

2 Rhoda went to the door in response to the knocking (Acts 12:13).

³The saints were praying for Peter, who had been cast into prison by Herod, and whose life was in danger (Acts 12:1-5).

⁴The girl became so excited when she recognized Peter's voice that she forgot to open the door. When she ran back into the house and told the saints, they thought she must be mad (Acts 12:14-15).

⁵Though they were praying for Peter, they were astonished to learn that he was free (Acts 12:16).

30. The apostle John—Matt. 4:21-22

¹John derives his importance to us only from his connection with Jesus Christ. It appears that he was, in fact, a blood relative of Jesus. This conclusion is drawn from a comparative reading of Matthew 27:56, Mark 15:40 and John 19:25. Assuming that all three writers refer to the same women who were present with Jesus at the crucifixion, we may conclude that "Salome," named by Mark, is "the mother of Zebedee's children" in Matthew's account, and is identified as Jesus' "mother's sister" in John's own writing. Thus John, who is one of "Zebedee's children" (Matt. 4:21), would be a first cousin of Jesus. Of course, this cannot be established as a certainty, but it might help to account for Jesus' apparent partiality toward John, who identifies himself as "the disciple whom Jesus loved" (John 21:20, 24).

²John's brother, James, was executed by Herod Agrippa; he was the first of the apostles to die a martyr's death (Acts 12:1-2). According to commonly accepted tradition, John outlived all the rest.

³"When Jesus therefore saw his mother, and the disciple standing by, whom he loved, he saith unto his mother, 'Woman, behold thy son!' Then saith he to the disciple, 'Behold thy mother!' And from that hour that disciple took her unto his own home" (John 19:26-27). This transaction would seem to strengthen the theory of a family tie: the brothers of Jesus being yet unbelieving (John 7:5), it would be quite normal for him to bequeath the care of his mother to a nephew, the next closest responsible male relative. (Cf. I Tim 5:4—"if any widow have

children or nephews, let them learn first to show piety at home, and to requite their parents. . . .")

[4]ZEBEDEE. It rhymes with "be," in the second line of the jingle.

31. Adam, the first man

[1]Adam and his wife, Eve, were the first parents of the human race (Gen. 1:27-28; 4:1).

[2]Noah shares with Adam the distinction of being a direct ancestor of every human being now living (Gen. 6:13; 7:21; 9:1).

[3]He was the original human being; he alone was made directly from the dust of the earth and vitalized by the breath of God (Gen. 2:7).

[4]He was the first man; he was not the first living creature that God made (Gen. 1:20-27).

[5]Oddly enough, Adam has no namesake in the Bible. We read of "the city Adam" (John 3:16), but no other man bears his name. However, in a figure, Christ is called "the last Adam" (I Cor. 15:45-47).

[6]Eve's deception at the hands of the serpent ushered sin into the world, with its attendant hardships upon the human race (Gen. 3:1-6, 16-19, 23-24). Their son, Cain, amplified the woe by the murder of his brother (Gen. 4:8).

[7]Adam, presumably full-grown at the time of his creation, was the youngest adult man who ever lived.

32. Enoch, the righteous patriarch—Genesis 5:21-24

[1]Enoch was "translated that he should not see death" (Heb. 11:5) at the age of 365; before that, he "walked with God" (Gen. 5:23-24). He was the only man of early times who did not experience death.

[2]Enoch was "the seventh from Adam." Many of these seven generations were still living when God took him from the earth. At least some of them were wicked, and Enoch prophesied that

the Lord would come and judge them, along with all the ungodly (Jude 14-15).

³"Behold, the Lord cometh with ten thousands of his saints" (Jude 14-b).

⁴"To convince all that are ungodly among them of all their ungodly deeds" (Jude 15).

⁵The coming of the Lord will be not only to punish the wicked, but to receive the righteous to glory (John 14:1-6; II Tim. 4:8).

33. Simeon, who blessed
the infant Jesus—Luke 2:25-35

¹Because no scriptures cover the time between Malachi and the coming of John the Baptist, it is often assumed that no divine revelations were given during that period.

²It is said of Simeon, "the Holy Ghost was upon him" (Luke 2:25). Not only had he had a prior revelation of the coming Christ (2:26), but he was guided by the Spirit to the temple at the proper time to see him (2:27) and blessed him with words of prophetic inspiration (Luke 2:32-35). Further evidence of inspirational endowment during the time between the Testaments is seen in the fact that the aged Anna, who "departed not from the temple," was known as a prophetess (Luke 2:36-38). Furthermore, the reaction of the worshipers at the temple to the experience of Zacharias would seem to indicate that visions were not uncommon (Luke 1:21).

³A free paraphrase of Simeon's exultation (Luke 2:30-32).

⁴He took the child in his arms as he spoke.

⁵He foretold the child's fulfillment of Old Testament prophecy (Isa. 42:6; 49:6).

⁶"the fall and rising again of many in Israel" (Luke 2:34).

⁷"the glory" (Luke 2:32).

⁸"a sword shall pierce through thy own soul" (Luke 2:35).

⁹Joseph and Mary "marvelled at those things which were spoken of him" (Luke 2:33). Though both had been alerted by prior

angelic announcement concerning the extraordinary child Jesus (Luke 1:26-33; Matt. 1:19-23), they continually failed to comprehend (Cf. Luke 2:48-51).

34. The Israelites under the leadership of Joshua

[1]The children of Israel crossed the Jordan (Josh. 3:14-17) and began the conquest of the rugged country of Canaan. The towns or cities allotted to the several tribes are listed in Joshua 15-21.

[2]The conquest of Canaan took about seven years, judging from Caleb's remarks about his own age in Joshua 14:6-13. He had been forty at the time of his spying mission. Thirty-eight years had then elapsed before the beginning of the conquest (Deut. 2:14-25). Since he was 85 when the tribal allotments were made, the conquest must have taken about seven years. The campaign involved a great deal of marching, taking the troops to all parts of the country. The battles in central and southern areas are related in Joshua, chapter 10; the northern campaign is summarized in chapter 11.

[3]Joshua's forces were of the generation which had grown up during the 40-year wilderness wandering, their seniors having perished during the march because of rebellion (Num. 14:26-35; Deut. 2:14) Joshua himself, along with Caleb, had survived (Num. 14:36-38), and had succeeded Moses as the leader of the nation (Josh. 1:1-9). As Caleb was in his eighties during the conquest (Josh. 14:10), Joshua, as Moses' attendant and military commander from the time of the Exodus (Exod. 17:8-13), must have been even older.

[4]See Numbers 27:18; Deuteronomy 34:9.

[5]To obey God it was necessary to obey Joshua (Num. 27:20; Josh. 1:5).

[6]Abraham, Isaac and Jacob, ancestors of the Israelites, had been "sojourners" in the land of Canaan (Gen. 17:8; Heb. 11:8-9). Their children were now inheriting it, as God had promised (Deut. 1:8; Josh. 21:43-45).

35. Joseph, son of Jacob, who became prime minister of Egypt

[1]The two most common roads to power and greatness in his day were military prowess and livestock holdings. He shows no record of having either.

[2]He was the second ruler of Egypt, next to Pharaoh (Gen. 41:39-41). He had jewelry of gold (41:42), a chariot of state (41:43), a house with banqueting facilities (43:16, 24-34), and a staff of servants (44:1).

[3]"the Lord was with Joseph" (Gen. 39:2). He was "a man in whom the spirit of God is" (Gen. 41:38).

[4]In his youth he had been a "tattle-tale:" "Joseph, being seventeen years old, was feeding the flock with his brethren . . . and Joseph brought unto his father their evil report" (Gen. 37:2). This may have been a factor, besides his father's favoritism, in the cause of the brothers' hatred toward him.

[5]In his youth he seemed to enjoy taunting his brothers with his dreams of future superiority (Gen. 37:5-11). His years of wrongful slavery and false imprisonment taught him humility (Gen. 41:16) and gentleness of spirit (Gen. 50:15-21).

[6]Both his own family (Gen. 45:6-8) and many countries relied upon Egypt's reserve of food supplies during the famine (Gen. 41:53-57).

[7]She was of the priestly class (Gen. 41:45).

[8]As already noted above.

[9]The treachery of his brothers, who sold him into slavery (Gen. 37:18); the spite of Potiphar's wife, who caused him to be sent to prison (Gen. 39:7-20); the ingratitude of the king's butler who forgot his favor to him (Gen. 40:1-23). The completeness of his triumph is reflected in the names which he gave to two sons: Manasseh, "causing forgetfulness;" "For God, said he, hath made me forget all my toil, and all my father's house" (Gen. 41:51); and Ephriam, "doubly fruitful; "For God hath caused me to be fruitful in the land of my affliction" (41:52).

36. Deborah, prophetess and judge of Israel

1 "Deborah," especially in its diminutive form, "Debbie," is one of the more popular names for girls today.

2 As a judge, whe enjoyed the favor of her people; she is famous as the only female judge, and surely the "Song of Deborah," of Judges 5, demonstrates a talent, whether literary or musical.

3 She was a prophetess (Judg. 4:4-5).

4 She was a prophetess—not a prophet; a woman—not a man.

5 Barak, the commander of Israel's warriors, besought her to accompany him into battle against the Canaanites (Judg. 4:6-8).

6 She consented, but warned that the enemy commander would be vanquished by a woman (Judg. 4:9).

7 The army was commanded by God to assemble on Mount Tabor (Judg. 4:6).

8 The battle took place in the valley of the river Kishon (Judg. 4:13-14).

9 The Israelites numbered ten thousand men (Judg. 4:14), and were virtually without military equipment (5:8); the Canaanites had a "multitude," a "host," reinforced by nine hundred chariots of iron (4:7, 13, 15). But the Israelites relied on the strength of God (4:6, 14; 5:1-3).

10 "They fought from heaven; the stars in their courses fought against Sisera" (Judg. 5:20).

11 During the days of the Canaanite oppression, it had been unsafe to travel: "the highways were unoccupied, and the travellers walked through by-ways" (Judg. 5:6). After Deborah's victory people could "walk by the way" (5:10) and gather for conversation at watering places without fear of the archers (5:11).

37. One of Peter's prison guards—Acts 12:1-19

[1] He was in the prison as a guard, not as an inmate (Acts 12:4).

[2] He and another soldier apparently had Peter chained to them (Acts 12:6).

[3] The angel of the Lord released Peter's chains, thereby severing the guards' bonds to him, too. Their duty would have been to prevent this if they could (Acts 12:8).

[4] The same chain that hindered Peter's movements also would hamper those of his guard.

[5] He had to stand trial before the king for allowing his prisoner to escape (Acts 12:19).

[6] He was executed for something he did not do and could not have prevented; it was the work of an angel of God (Acts 12:7, 19).

[7] The guards apparently were asleep when Peter was miraculously released (Acts 12:6, 10, 18).

[8] Herod had them all put to death (Acts 12:19).

38. The High Priest under the Law of Moses

[1] The high priest's robe had golden bells around the hemline (Exod. 28:31-35).

[2] He wore precious stones upon his breast (Exod. 28:15-21).

[3] Like other provisions of the old covenant (Col. 2:17), the high priest was a shadow of things to come, a type of Jesus Christ (Heb. 9:9-11; 10:1).

[4] The sound of his bells was mandatory; the penalty for silence was death (Exod. 28:35). His fragrance was due to an exclusive perfume with which he was anointed (Exod. 30:22-37). And, since he held office only during his earthly lifetime (Heb. 7:23), he was visible.

[5] The former was true because of the aforementioned fragrance, the latter, because of his distinctive clothing (Exod. 28:1-39; 29:4-7).

[6]The priest, according to law, had to be a lineal descendant of Aaron, the brother of Moses (Exod. 29:9, 29-30). Even Jesus, the Son of God, because of his fleshly descent through another tribe, could not become God's High Priest until the law was changed (Heb. 7:11-28).

39. The prophet Balaam, son of Beor

[1]Balaam was engaged by the Moabites to curse the children of Israel (Num. 22:4-7). His "star" prophecy is recorded in Numbers 24:17: "There shall come a Star out of Jacob, . . . and shall smite the corners of Moab." It was fulfilled by David's conquest (II Sam. 8:2).

[2]"And the Lord put a word in Balaam's mouth . . .;" Balaam described himself as "the man whose eyes are open" (Num. 23:5; 24:3, 15).

[3]His words were those of inspiration, in support of God's will and plans for Israel (Cf. Num. 23:7-10, 18-24; 24:3-9).

[4]Though he could not deliver the curse for which Balak offered to pay him (Num. 22:7, 17-18), he earned his money by proposing a plan which would cause the Israelites to bring God's wrath upon themselves (Cf. Num. 31:16; II Peter 2:15; Jude 11; Rev. 2:14).

[5]The plan involved Israel in social, sexual and religious relationships with the heathen Moabites and Midianites (Num. 25:1-9).

40. Elisha, the prophet

[1]We first meet Elisha as he plows his father's field. The fact that he has twelve yoke of oxen before him would seem to imply some affluence (I Kings 19:19).

[2]When he first left his oxen to follow Elijah, the old prophet said to him, "Go back again: for what have I done to thee?" (I Kings 19:20). Years later, when Elijah was about to be taken from the earth, he tried three times to discourage Elisha from accompanying him (II Kings 2:2, 4, 6).

³ Elisha refused to be left behind, and was ultimately rewarded by having his ambition realized: that of acceding to his master's power and position as the prophet of God (II Kings 2:9-10, 13-15).

⁴ Ben-hadad, king of Syria, sent to inquire of Elisha whether he should recover from his illness. The prophet replied, "Thou mayest certainly recover," which meant simply that the king should not die of his illness. He didn't; he was murdered by the messenger, as Elisha had predicted. The messenger himself then became king (II Kings 8:7-15).

⁵ He served his apprenticeship as servant to Elijah, who was described as "an hairy man" (II Kings 1:8).

⁶ His servant, Gehazi, was smitten with leprosy and became "as white as snow" (II Kings 5:20-27).

⁷ Whereas Gehazi was cursed for his greed for wealth, Elisha's hunger was for "a double portion" of the Spirit that had been upon Elijah, that is, the Spirit of God (II Kings 2:9).

⁸ The exploits of Elisha were certainly no less remarkable than those of his predecessor, even extending beyond his death (Cf. II Kings 13:20-21).

⁹ We see Elisha in what might be called the role of a cook as he corrects the recipe of the sons of the prophets in II Kings 4:38-41. He plays the role of "army engineer" as he designs a system of ditches to supply water to Jehoshaphat's stranded troops (II Kings 3:9-20). He is seen as adviser to the king in II Kings 6:9-10 and other places. The case of Naaman the leper reveals him as a healer of disease (II Kings 5:1-14). An example of his work as a predictor of the future is found in II Kings 7:1-20.

¹⁰ The king of Syria once sent a detachment of soldiers to capture Elisha and bring him to Damascus (II Kings 6:11-15).

¹¹ When his would-be abductors arrived, Elisha asked the Lord to smite them with blindness, whereupon he led them, helpless into the hands of the king of Israel; then, upon opening their eyes so that they might see their hopeless condition, he had them fed as honored guests and sent them home unharmed.

As a result of this gesture of mercy, there was a long period of peace between Israel and Syria (II Kings 6:18-23).

12 An allusion to the occasion when Elisha came to the aid of a young prophet who had accidentally dropped a borrowed axe into the river. Elisha restored the borrowed property by causing the iron axehead to float to the surface (II Kings 6:1-7).

13 God had told the prophet Elijah, "I have left me seven thousand in Israel, all the knees which have not bowed unto Baal, and every mouth which hath not kissed him" (I Kings 19:18). Elisha was one of that remnant.

41. The apostle Matthew

1 Matthew's former occupation was that of publican, a collector of custom (Luke 5:27; Matt. 9:9). His work, then, would include the counting ("telling") of tolls, or duty assessments.

2 He became a disciple of Jesus, with a special commission to preach (Mark 3:14-17), or to "tell souls" the good news of salvation through Christ.

3 He also wrote the gospel account which bears his name, which, as inspired Scripture, is "able to make thee [men] wise unto salvation through faith which is in Christ Jesus" (II Tim. 3:15). This assuredly is a higher purpose than that of his former vocation.

4 The other gospel writers refer to him as "Levi" at the time of his calling (Mark 2:14; Luke 5:27-29), but after he becomes a disciple he is always called "Matthew." With his new life, he received a new name.

5 The disrepute in which his fellow Jews held all publicans (Matt. 9:11).

6 The suffering of shame for the name of Christ (Acts 5:41; Heb. 12:2).

7 "Blessed are ye, when men shall revile you, and persecute you, and shall say all manner of evil against you falsely, for my sake" (Matt. 5:11).

81

[8]"for great is your reward in heaven" (Matt. 5:12). See also Matthew 10:28.

42. Zipporah, Moses' wife, daughter of the priest of Midian—Exodus 2:16-22

[1]Her father, Reuel (also known as "Raguel" and as Jethro), had seven daughters (Exod. 2:16) and a son (Num. 10:29).

[2]Her marriage to Moses (Exod. 2:21), God's lawgiver, lifted her from obscurity and made her name a household word among Bible readers.

[3]Moses said, "I have been a stranger in a strange land" (Exod. 2:22).

[4]Their reunion is related in Exodus 18:1-6.

[5]Moses was threatened with divine wrath for his failure to circumcise their son. Zipporah quickly performed the operation, whereupon her husband's life was spared. Her scolding words to him are recorded as part of the narrative (Exod. 4:24-26).

43. Barnabas, missionary partner of Paul

[1]Dropping the musical jargon, the idea is simply that, in the Lord's plan to evangelize the world, there was an important need of the right kind of man to "play second fiddle" to a more prominent personage.

[2]Barnabas was such a man. He owned land (Acts 4:36-37). His compassion is seen in his generous gift for distribution to the needy (Acts 4:34-37), his intercession for the converted Saul of Tarsus (Acts 9:26-27), and his willingness to give the young John Mark a second opportunity (Acts 15:36-39).

[3]Barnabas was "a good man, and full of the Holy Ghost and of faith," as a result of which, as he taught, "much people was added unto the Lord" (Acts 11:24, 26).

[4]The Lord used Barnabas' talents to lead and train the budding new convert, Saul of Tarsus, until the latter outstripped him and

came to the front as Paul the apostle (Acts 11:22-26, 30; 13:2; cf. 13:13). /

[5]Paul soon overshadowed his earlier sponsor and, whenever the two names appear together in later references, his, not that of Barnabas, is usually mentioned first (Acts 13:13, 50), as Paul had become "the chief speaker" (Acts 14:12). When the two eventually parted company, the Bible narrative follows the exploits of Paul rather than those of Barnabas (Acts 15:39-41).

44. Ebed-melech, the Ethiopian eunuch who rescued Jeremiah from the dungeon

[1]"Now when Ebed-melech the Ethiopian . . . heard that they had put Jeremiah in the dungeon; . . . (he) went forth . . . and spake unto the king, saying, My lord the king, these men have done evil in all that they have done to Jeremiah the prophet, whom they have cast into the dungeon; and he is like to die for hunger in the place where he is" (Jer. 38:7-9).

[2]By the king's leave, Ebed-melech drew Jeremiah up out of the dungeon with cords, having given his "old cast clouts and old rotten rags" to pad himself against the cutting ropes (Jer. 38:10-13).

[3]Jeremiah was the victim of plots by the false prophets and rebellious priests of Judah (Jer. 26:7-9). Ebed-melech was an Ethiopian (Jer. 38:7).

[4]God promised the Ethiopian that his life would be spared when the army of Babylon captured Jerusalem, an occasion which saw the slaughter of many of the people of Judah, including the children of the king (Jer. 39:15-18; 39:6).

45. Absalom, rebel son of David—II Samuel 13-18

[1]Absalom arranged the death of his half-brother, Amnon, to avenge the rape of his sister Tamar. He then fled the country, taking refuge with his maternal grandfather, Talmai, the king of Geshur (II Sam. 13:28-38; I Chron. 3:1-2). Geshur was a small

kingdom beyond the Jordan and to the north of Gilead (Deut. 3:13-14).

2"now Absalom in his lifetime had taken and reared up for himself a pillar, which is in the king's dale: for he said, I have no son to keep my name in remembrance: And he called the pillar after his own name: and it is called unto this day Absalom's place" (II Sam. 18:18).

3In the best manner of an ambitious politician, Absalom won the people's hearts and undermined their faith in his father's justice by his own exaggerated personal concern for their problems (II Sam. 15:2-6).

4His own heart became the target for the three deadly darts of Joab (II Sam. 18:14).

5Absalom and his army had pursued his father David across the Jordan, where they fought a great battle in the wood of Ephraim. He was mounted on a mule (II Sam. 17:24; 18:6-9).

6Absalom's mule ran under a low-hanging oak tree, leaving the rider hanging helplessly in midair with his head caught in the branches, utterly defenseless against the vengeful Joab and his darts (II Sam. 18:9-17).

7"In all Israel there was none to be so much praised as Absalom for his beauty. . . ." (II Sam. 17:25; 19:11-13; I Chron. 2:13-16.)

8Absalom's popularity with others seems to have been exceeded only by his opinion of himself (Cf. II Sam. 18:18).

9Hung it in the tree, that is, as cited above.

46. Abigail, one of David's wives,
    formerly the wife of Nabal

1David, in a rage at Nabal over the latter's ungracious reception of his messengers, was on his way to kill him. Nabal's wife, Abigail, soothed David's anger and won his friendship by supplying him with an abundance of choice foodstuff (I Sam. 25:1-35).

²When Nabal learned of his narrow escape and how his wife had saved him, he suffered a coronary attack and died (I Sam. 25:36-38). Shortly afterward David, the "chosen of the Lord" (I Sam. 16:10-12) made Abigail his own wife (I Sam. 25:39-42).

³David was, of course, of the tribe of Judah. So also had been her first husband, being of the house of Caleb (I Sam. 25:3; I Chron. 2:3-5, 9, 18).

⁴Nabal had died, as related above.

⁵David also had a sister named Abigail (I Chron. 2:13-16).

⁶Her son was named Daniel (I Chron. 3:1)

⁷She, along with the rest of David's family, was taken prisoner by raiding Amalekites during her husband's absence. David pursued them with 400 of his 600 travel-weary troops and liberated them and other captives (I Sam. 30:1-18).

⁸She saved Nabal's life, as related above.

⁹Her timely intervention kept David from becoming a murderer (I Sam. 25:32-34).

47. Micah, the Ephraimite who stole money from his mother—Judges 17-18

¹He hired a young Levite to be "a father and a priest" to his household (Judg. 17:7-10). "and the young man was unto him as one of his sons" (Judg. 17:11).

²His priest accepted an offer of a more prestigious job, that of priest to the northern segment of the tribe of Dan (Judg. 18:19-20).

³All he got for his trouble was a threat against his life (Judg. 18:22-26).

⁴The mercenary priest's name was Jonathan (Judg. 18:30). Certainly the later Jonathan, the selfless friend of David, was a greater man than this one (II Sam. 1:17-27).

⁵Micah was an idolater (Judg. 17:3-5).

⁶He respected God enough to want a Levitical priest (Judg. 17:12-13). But he mixed his worship to God with the afore-mentioned idolatry, specifically transgressing the first and second commandments of the law of Moses (Judg. 17:5; 18:13-14, 24; Exod. 20:1-4).

⁷His name was Micah (Judg. 17:1); he was hardly worthy to be compared to the faithful prophet Micah, who lived much later (Mic. 1:1).

48. The prophet Samuel

¹Samuel would be distinctive for his long hair. He was under a vow imposed by his mother before he was born: "I will give him unto the Lord all the days of his life, and there shall no razor come upon his head" (I Sam. 1:11).

²After he went to live with Eli the priest, his mother "made him a little coat, and brought it to him from year to year" (I Sam. 2:19).

³It seems apparent from the account of Samuel's divine call that the boy slept in "the temple of the Lord" (I Sam. 3:1-5, 15), which was at that time, and until much later, the tabernacle, or tent, that Moses had built in the wilderness (Cf. I Chron. 15:1; II Sam. 7:2). The boy Samuel "ministered unto the Lord" (I Sam. 3:1). One of his duties was to open the doors of the house of worship each morning (3:15).

⁴The Lord added to the child's responsibilities that of prophetically declaring the doom of Eli's house, a task which the boy was reluctant to do (3:10-15).

⁵What reader has not been charmed by the account of Samuel's birth and childhood?

⁶Samuel served the Lord all the days of his life (I Sam. 2:18; I Sam. 7:15-17), and was even called back from the grave to render service as a prophet (I Sam. 28:7-20).

⁷Samuel summoned his people to a revival gathering at Mizpeh. The Philistines, mistaking the religious service for a counsel of

war, attacked the Israelites while Samuel was offering prayers and sacrifice (I Sam. 7:3-10).

8 God led the Israelites against their enemies (I Sam. 7:10), and the Philistines were so badly beaten that "they came no more into the coast of Israel," and remained subdued "all the days of Samuel" (7:11-14)—presumably until the kingdom of Saul was founded. In other words, there were no enemies for a long time.

9 Samuel was the last of the judges (I Sam. 8:3-7), the first of the great oral prophets; "all Israel from Dan even to Beer-sheba" knew of him (I Sam. 3:20).

10 Samuel's grandson, Heman, became the head of a line of temple musicians (I Chron. 6:33; 15:17; 25:5-6).

11 That is, he recorded the laws of the kingdom of Israel: "Then Samuel told the people the manner of the kingdom, and wrote it in a book, and laid it up before the Lord" (I Sam. 10:25).

49. Abner, uncle of King Saul and commander of his army

1 A free paraphrase of Abner's warning to Asahel, who was pursuing him after a skirmish between the forces of David and those of the house of Saul: "Turn thee aside from following me: wherefore should I smite thee to the ground?" (II Sam. 2:22).

2 His father's name was Ner; the son was Ab-ner (I Sam. 14:50).

3 Ner's claim to fame lies in the notoriety of his son and, more remotely, that of his grandson, Saul. Were it not for the oft-repeated phrase, "Abner, the son of Ner," the Bible reader would hardly be aware of Ner's existence.

4 The sportscast is narrated in II Samuel 2:12-16: "And Abner the son of Ner, and the servants of Ishbosheth the son of Saul, went out from Mahanaim to Gibeon: And Joab the son of Zeruiah, and the servants of David, went out, and met together by the pool of Gibeon: and they sat down, the one on the one side of the pool, and the other on the other side of the pool. And

87

Abner said to Joab, Let the young men now arise, and play before us. And Joab said, Let them arise. Then there arose . . . twelve of Benjamin, . . . and twelve of the servants of David. And they caught every one his fellow by the head, and thrust his sword in his fellow's side; so they fell down together."

[5]Remember the famous comic strip, "Li'l Abner"?

50. Ahithophel, traitorous counselor of King David

[1]Ahithophel lived in the city of Giloh (II Sam. 15:12).

[2]He was counselor to the king—a member of the royal court (II Sam. 15:12).

[3]He hanged himself (II Sam. 17:23).

[4]He took his own life because Absalom and the elders of Israel followed the advice of another instead of his. His death, of course, guaranteed that such a humiliating thing should never happen again (Cf. II Sam. 17:1-23).

[5]"Ahithophel" will complete the rhyme of the last line.